SHINING LIGHTS
of the
REFORMATION

DESLEE CAMPBELL

Memorable Christians Book 3

Table of Contents

Chapter 1

William Tyndale (c.1494-1536)

The Reformation of the 16th century was a watershed period of human history, just as the 4th century had been, when Constantine the Great, the first Christian emperor, was baptised and when Christianity became the official religion of Rome, in 380. Reformation meant change for the better: a period of spiritual and intellectual contesting, redefinition and the discarding of error and outdated ways. Rome responded at that time with its own attempts at reform: called the Counter- Reformation or Catholic Reformation and has gradually, very gradually, come to agree with the Reformers in many ways, for example Rome no longer burns heretics, the Mass is said in local languages and the laity may read the Bible for themselves.

This book hopefully encourages others as we are entering another watershed period of human history in which the same courage, earnest study of the Scriptures and reliance upon God that the Reformers exhibited will be needed. Shining lights will continue to be important guides and leaders in the Church.

This book is a useful brief summary of the Reformation Era for students. It picks up Western Christian history at a point where the faith had spread in the Western World and had penetrated successfully. In order to achieve this, however, and to ensure ongoing compliance, the Latin speaking Church had resorted to persecuting and suppressing all other forms of Christian faith and all dissent, and resorted to harsh and unchristian methods, the most notorious of which were the numerous Inquisitions. At the same time Roman Catholic leadership was permeated by such evils as financial extortion of the poor, political infighting, manipulation, intrigues, brutality, poor leadership, nepotism, fornication and even murder. Some Popes were evil men who were generally old (and they virtually always died in office) so that even the best of them were in their dotage during much of their reigns. This enabled unscrupulous underlings to literally 'get away with murder', and other evils.

Martin Luther said that the church *"is spoiled and robbed by the princes and prelates, they give nothing but take and steal..... the church is more torn and tattered than a beggar's cloak"*.[1]

Therefore many of the shining lights discussed below were dedicated to challenging the Church by comparing it with the Christianity of the New Testament. But in order to do this they had to know what the Bible said, which was a considerable challenge when only academics and some monastics could read the Koine Greek of the New Testament or St Jerome's Latin Vulgate text. Many people were not even literate in their mother tongue and the Bible was only really available in Latin anyway. Add to this was the fact that lay people were forbidden to read it, and certainly were not permitted to interpret it for themselves. All of this is why most of the bright lights of the Reformation were either monks and priest, or academics, or a combination all three. It fell to a monk who taught in a university to lead the charge against the errors into which the Church had fallen and to reveal those closed secrets to Europe. His story is in the first chapter. His name was Martin Luther.

There had been Protestants before the Protestant reformation. The Inquisitions would not have been nearly so busy if this had not been the case: people like Johann Huss, who dared to translate the Bible and was burned as a heretic.

Because Scripture is the basis of the Christian faith and because it was important that it was available in the language people used daily, the chapter on the Bible translator William Tyndale (previously published in my *Bright Shining Lights of a Previous Era*, 2020/2024) is reshaped for this chapter. Tyndale was described by Peter Hammond as 'the Morning Star of the Reformation'[2] so Tyndale's biography is a good place to start. Translations of Scripture into English (by Tyndale) and into

German (by Luther) and their ready reproduction using the printing press enabled reformist ideas to be spread.

Like John Wycliffe, but about a century and a half later, William Tyndale translated the Bible into English. He had a distinct advantage compared with earlier translators: technological progress. William Caxton had invented a printing press in 1477, so that Tyndale's Bible could be reproduced in unlimited numbers and distributed widely, whereas John Wycliffe's Bible (for example) had to be hand written.

William Tyndale was born in about 1495 to a Welsh family in Gloucestershire, England, making him a decade younger than Martin Luther. He attended Oxford University and was awarded an M.A. at the young age of 21. He then went to Cambridge University, studying Greek under the great Renaissance scholar, Erasmus of Rottersdam (c.1466-1536), who, in 1516, himself had translated the Greek New Testament into Classical Latin, which only well educated people could read.[3]

Plate 0.1. William Tyndale. Public domain.

In 1524, when the Bishop of London refused to support Tyndale's plan to translate the whole Bible into English, he went to Hamburg, in Germany, where he consulted with Martin Luther, who had translated the Bible into German.[4] Tyndale, a brilliant linguist, spoke eight languages. Thesse included Hebrew and Greek, which enabled him to translate directly from the original languages into every-day English. He completed the translation of the New Testament in a year and made constant revisions until 1535. He had translated from the original languages, whereas John Wycliffe had translated from St Jerome's 4th century Latin translation, which was based upon the original but was less accurate.

Using a printing press, copies of Tyndale's text were made in Worms, in Germany, and smuggled into England where they were in great demand, although the authorities had siezed, confiscated and publicly burned them. At that time only clergy were considered qualified to read the Word of God and translations in English were suppressed because they opened the Bible up to the laity (and even women).[5]

In May of 1535 Henry Phillips, supposedly a close friend of William Tyndale, betrayed him to royal officials at Vilvord, near Brussels, and he was tried, and convicted of treason and heresy. Tyndale was held in prison for almost 17 months, during which time he continued his work. Then he was strangled and burnt at the stake. His last words were, *"Lord, open the king of England's eyes"* and three years later King Henry VIII sanctioned the printing of the Great Bible in England.[6]

The Great Bible was the work of the linguist and priest Miles Coverdale (1488-1568) who had worked with William Tyndale in Hamburg (Germany) in 1529, and who was able to complete The Great Bible in 1539. After Tyndale's martyrdom, Coverdale, whose own life was often in danger, was able to complete those parts of the Old Testament that Tyndale had left incomplete. Their work remains the basis of the English language Authorised Version and the Revised Version.

Alhough Shakespeare receives much of the credit for creating 'the Queen's English' far more credit should go to the linguistic skills of William Tyndale,[7] but the greatest result of the Tyndale-Coverdale collaboration was that any literate English person could now read and understand the Scriptures and so test Reformation doctrines for themselves.

Chapter 1

Martin Luther (1483-1546)

The European Reformation is notionally dated from October 31, 1517, when the German Augustinian monk and academic, Martin Luther, apparently attached his ninety-five theses or beliefs upon the door of the Castle Church of Wittenberg.[8]

Luther's father had planned a career in the Law for him and Luther had gained a Master of Arts from the University of Erfurt. Luther's life was changed by a dramatic event on July 2, 1505. He was caught in a thunderstorm and flung to the ground, vowing that, if he survived, he would become a monk. It was a mere two weeks later that, despite his father's opposition, he entered the Reformed Congregation of the Eremetical Order of St Augustine in Erfurt.[9] Perhaps he was deeply anxious about his soul's salvation and, certainly, at that time a religious vocation was considered the surest way to gain merit for eternity. Luther was first ordained in lower orders in 1506, and ordained a priest in 1507. He was sent to Rome in 1510 and became a Doctor of Theology in 1512 after which he taught Biblical studies at the new University of Wittenberg. Through intense study of the Scriptures, Luther came to the understanding that righteousness and salvation were gifts from God through unmerited mercy.[10]

Meanwhile others were coming to similar conclusions because all of this soul-searching did not arise in a religious vacuum. As early as the twelfth century, and much to the annoyance of local parish priests and bishops, friars and other popular preachers[11] had actively and eloquently preached against such Catholic practices as infant baptism, images and crucifixes, corrupt clergy and the excessive wealth of the church. Erasmus of Rotterdam (c.1469-1536) and other humanists and

Renaissance philosophers had also questioned Catholic dogma and clerical power.

In 1518 the young scholar, Philip Melanchthon (1497-1560) became professor of Greek at Wittenberg University; becoming Luther's firmest supporter and friend, although they were very different personalities.[12] Luther was a robust, well-built man with a big personality, bombastic and passionate whereas Melanchthon was small, timid, scholarly, reserved, cautious and conciliatory.

Luther was particularly upset when the Archbishop of Brandenburg (who actually held three sees)[13] claimed in a pamphlet that indulgences not only reduced one's time in purgatory but also had the power to forgive sin; an innovative piece of doctrine. Luther was oppose to any doctrine that could not be supported by Scripture and was certainly opposed to the selling of indulgence,[14] especially by the eloquent Dominican friar, Johann Tetzel [1470-1519] who was selling them nearby (mainly because Pope Leo X was addicted to lavish spending and building projects). In 1518 Pope Leo sent Karl von Miltitz, a young Saxon nobleman in lower orders, to visit both the pious Elector Frederick of Saxony and Luther on a mission of conciliation. He found Luther humble and ready to make concessions so he went to Leipzig to meet with Tetzel, "*reproved him for excesses, accused him of mendacity and embezzlement, and dismissed him.*" Tetzel retired to his monastery and died in August, 1519, but Luther had written him a kind letter saying that indulgences were not the cause of his quarrel with Rome: "*the child had quite another father*".[15]

The Pope supported the Archbishop and, in 1519, Luther had to debate against the professor of theology at the University of Ingolstadt, Johann of Eck (1486-1543) who reminded him of how and why the Bohemian, Johann Huss (1369-1415) had been killed and called Luther's ideas "*Bohemian poison*". From then on, Eck became his relentless adversary.[16] When Luther had read Johann Huss's opinions and found that he agreed with them, danger seemed very real as Huss had been burnt as a heretic over a century previously.[17]

From his reading of the Scriptures, Luther developed teachings that included: justification by faith alone (not at all by good works), the priesthood of all believers, opposition to the cult of saints and the denied of papal primacy. Luther opposed pilgrimages, clerical celibacy, Masses for the dead, monastic vows and communion of only the bread, rather than the two kinds. Luther's 95 theses circulated widely in German and Latin and a pamphlet war broke out as Tetzel produced his own theses about papal authority[18] and Johann of Eck joined the fray with his own pamphlet, *Obelisci* (Obesisks) in March, 1518, which challenged Luther's theses.

Plate 1.1.

Martin Luther by Cranach the Elder (1526). Public domain.

Another Professor of Wittenberg, Andreas Bodenstein of Carlstadt, who became a supporter of Luther, defended Luther's 95 theses and incidentally claimed the paramount authority of the Bible over tradition and papal decisions. When Eck challenged Carlstadt to a debate he agreed and drew up an agenda of thirteen items. The battle took place at Pleissenberg Castle with Eck clearly the superior so that Luther intervened with his brilliant and powerful skill. The debate raged over twelve days but EcK had tempted Luther into committing heresy. "*The Reformation now advanced from a minor dispute about indulgences to a major challenge of papal authority over Christendom*".[19]

Luther was charged with heresy and was threatened with excommunicated by the Papal Bull *Exsurge Domine* in 1520 but he publicly burned the bull at the gate of Wittenberg, like an ancient prophet.[20] He published three major articles,[21] which attacked the corrupt papacy (which he called the Anti-Christ) and the Latin Church (which he called Babylon). The pope could not ignore these. Luther was excommunicated on January 3, 1521 and summoned to the Diet of Worms (April, 1521) and was commanded to recant. He courageously stood before the assembly and made his famous declaration:

> *"Unless I am convicted by the testimony of the Scriptures and by clear reason (for I do not trust in the Pope or Councils alone since it is well known that they often erred and contradicted themselves) I am bound by the Scriptures I have quoted. My conscience is captive to the Word of God. I cannot and will not retract anything since it is neither safe nor right to go against my conscience. Here I stand. I cannot do otherwise. God help me. Amen".[22]*

The new Emperor, Charles V, placed Luther's works under an imperial ban but he survived by being kidnapped and secreted in the fortress of Wartburg Castle where he lived in disguise, protected by the Frederick the Wise (1463-1525) the Elector of Saxony.[23]

Lutheranism had spread to The Netherlands where Eck and Girolamo Alexander, Luther's dedicated opponents, published the Bill against him. They had his books publicly burned in Antwerp, Liège, Louvain and Cologne.[24]

While in hiding, Luther translated the New Testament into popular, readable German prose, a welcome and enduring achievement,[25] which also enhanced a sense of German identity and culture. Luther was recalled to Wittenberg in 1522 by the City Council to take control of the quickly deteriorating civil disorder, inflamed by radicals and extremists whose leaders included his former friend, Andreas of Carlstadt. Luther was enthusiastically welcomed and the old modes of worship were largely restored, which raised Luther's approval rating amongst the upper class. Luther was relatively conservative and wanted to make changes slowly. When he dispensed with Mass-priests and they had no income he proposed that clerical salaries be paid out of government coffers (which remains the case).[26]

In 1523 Luther showed sympathy for the Jews by writing "*That Jesus Christ was born a Jew*".[27] Later, however, probably because he had failed to make converts amongst the Jews, he also wrote the vicious tract "*Against the Jews and Their Lies*", which called for the burning of synagogues, Jewish homes, schools, Talmuds and prayer-books; which influenced the Lutheran public, as history would show.[28] Anti-semitism was the greatest stain on Luther's reputation.

Luther's teaching of *sola fide* (only faith) undermined much of the accumulated superstructure of Roman Catholic life which was designed to earn spiritual merit for one person or another, such as the purchase of indulgences and paying for Masses to be said to help the deceased to enter Heaven and the exertions of pilgrimages or self-flagellation to help oneself to get there. One of Luther's enduring achievements was to vindicate lay-life as the best field for God's service rather than the unnatural ascetic life.[29]

In 1525 Luther married an ex-nun, Katharine von Bora, in 1525. He fathered five or six children and had a happy married life. He also composed many memorable hymns and translated others from Latin into German, many of which are still sung. He also played the lute, sang well and taught his children to sing many of the hymns which he had composed.

Plate 1.2. Katharine Luther. Public domain.

In the last decades of Luther's life his energies were deflected from spreading Reformist teachings among the populace to scholarly debates and contests with his critics. Also, it is said that Luther spent as much time debating with other Reformation leaders on theological details as with the Catholic opposition.[30] These debates included with the great humanist, Erasmus (1466-1536) who conducted a pamphlet contest with Luther; the radical Carlstadt, who had tried to radicalise Wittenberg while Luther was in hiding; the Anabaptists and Thomas Münzer (c.1488-1425) *"a man of great originality and prophetic powers"*[31] who became a leader in the Peasants' Revolt (1524-1525). From 1530, the *Augsburg Confession* was compiled for the Emperor Charles, although it was largely the work of Melanchthon (and was more radical than Luther would have chosen).[32] It was read to the Emperor and the papal legate but Catholic theologians opposed it strenuously and demanded that the Protestants submit. Armed conflict seemed inevitable even though Luther had believed that it was immoral to fight against the Emperor. (He had opposed the Peasants' Revolt and when it was crushed with great bloodshed Luther's prestige among the lower classers fell.)

Political events converged to save Luther from martyrdom: Frederick 'the Wise' died and his brother John 'the Steadfast' (1525-1532) who was a Lutheran, vigorously protected him. At the time unity was desirable because a Turkish army had been victorious in Hungary (1526) [and soon besieged Vienna, in 1529][33]; a new pope, Clement VII (1523) had different priorities and, in any case, he became a prisoner of the Emperor in 1527; many German cities had become Lutheran and Philip of Hesse tried hard to bring the Protestant parties together so that the pro-Lutheran states formed the Schmalkalden League to fight if necessary. The Emperor Charles V chose to call a truce in 1532. Then he left Germany for Spain and Italy and more cities and territories joined the Lutherans.

From about 1520 the various Anabaptist groups were gaining adherents, despite being opposed by Luther, Calvin, Zwingli and all Roman Catholics. Their theology was so radical that they drew some of the heat away from Luther and yet multiplied despite their sufferings.

After Luther's death in 1546 there was war between various religious and political powers: the Emperor, German electors and France until the Peace of Augsburg was signed in 1555, which permanently allocated each territory as exclusively Catholic or Lutheran. Even the outward appearance of a united church had disappeared, which Melanchthon lived to see before he died in 1560; although Luther had already died.

Martin Luther was a complex character: often given to pessimism and depression and bouts of anger interspersed with periods of retreating from social contacts or, alternatively, dynamic preaching and debating. He held that every good that humanity could do was worthless as people (even those who were saved) were sinful - but the papacy was evil.[34] Although Luther wavered early in his battle, later he had stood, unmoved, in the middle ground, a towering figure but with arch-protestants opposing him on his left, Catholics constantly attacking at his back and a variety of radicals undermining him on his right.

Chapter 2

Philip Melanchthon (1497-1560)

Philip Melanchthon is the least well-known of the great lights of the Reformation but he was a leading intellectual and theologian and he closely collaborated with Martin Luther and deserves to be better known and understood.

Philip was born Philip Schwartzerdt (meaning 'black earth') in Brennen, Germany a city which was burned down by the French when Philip was about eleven years old (in 1507). He was introduced to Latin and Greek from the age of ten and a year later, after both of his grandfathers died, Philip went to live with his grandmother (whose brother, a noted Renaissance humanist, had changed the boy's name to the Greek name Melanchthon).

At the age of twelve Philip entered the University of Heidelberg to study rhetoric, philosophy, Greek and astronomy. He then studied at The University of Tübingen: medicine, mathematics, jurisprudence and astrology. He was awarded a Master of Arts in 1516 and began to study theology, gaining a bachelor's degree and he also lectured in Classics. In 1518, Martin Luther then arranged for Melanchthon to be invited to Wittenberg as Professor of Greek and he continued to study the New Testament, being strongly influenced by Luther. In turn, he helped Luther by organising Lutheran doctrines into a systematic and logical whole.[35] As most of the Reformers did, he married (in 1520). His wife, Katharina Krapp, the daughter of the Mayor of Wittenberg, gave birth to Anna, Philipp, Georg and Magdalen.[36]

As Melanchthon had come to theology via Classical languages and philosophy his approach was much influenced by humanism and, as he was of a gentle disposition, he sought mediation and conciliation rather than confrontation. Yet he was often embroiled in confrontation: at diets, synods and organised disputations (which were the talk-fests of the day). Some of these are as follows:

He attended the Leipzig Disputation (1519) and made provocative comments.

His views were attacked by Luther's adversary, Johann Eck, and Melanchthon responded with a written defence (1519).

He wrote a defence of Luther in 1521.

At the Diet of Speyer he opposed Zwingli's view of Holy Communion (1529).

At the Colloquy of Marburg (1529) Luther and Melanchthon tried to reconcile with Zwingli but could not reconcile their disagreement on Holy Communion.

At the Diet of Augsburg (1530) Melanchthon was a leading light and major contributor to the *Augsburg Confession*.[37] In 1521 Melanchthon published a small volume *Cardinal Points of Theology* (*Loci Communes*) which set out Luther's theology in a systematic and convenient way.

Plate 2.1.

Philip Melanchthon by Hans Holbein (c.1535). Public domain.

When Luther was secreted in Wartburg Castle (from 1521 to 1522) his protégé was the intellectual leader among the Reform Movement, and again for two decades after Luther had died in 1540, although he was unable to control the radicals and extremists who came to Wittenberg in 1521 to exert control over the city council. They destroyed images, confronted Catholicism, forbad beggary and ordered that the needy should be aided by the city.[38]

Academic theologians owe a great debt to Melanchthon as he first treated the Scriptures like he treated the Classics, with the same spirit of enquiry, the same academic discipline, consideration for historicity and openness to archaeological evidence.[39] As noted in the previous chapter, Philip Melanchthon and Martin Luther were very different in stature and in personality. Luther was practical man, a large and robust man who had great courage and determination whereas Melanchthon was small, timid, but sincere, loyal and dedicated and an excellent scholar. Perhaps Melanchthon is less well known because his light paled in the glare of Luther's radiance.

Chapter 3

Ulrich Zwingli (1484-1531)

Huldrych/Ulrich Zwingli was born in Switzerland and received a thorough education. He was ordained a Catholic priest in 1506 and pastored a church at Glarus. Here, as a dedicated follower of the Renaissance scholar, Erasmus, Zwingli devoted himself to learning Greek, studying the Church Father and pursuing humanistic studies. He also memorised St Paul's epistles by heart. Zwingli became a chaplain in the Swiss mercenaries who served the Pope. In 1518 he was elected minister in Zurich and his reform agenda was supported. He lived in Zurich for the rest of his life.[40]

In 1519 Zwingli preached sermons on the New Testament, which betrayed Protestant sentiments. This was two years after Luther had publicised his theses but Zwingli had arrived at his views independently through his profound scholarly efforts and his views varied from Luther's, especially on the nature of Holy Communion. He soon preached against such Roman Catholic doctrines as purgatory, monasticism and prayers to the saints and by 1522 he wrote against the authority of bishops and popes, which revealed that Zwingli had become a complete Protestant.

Plate 3.1. Ulrich Zwingli. Public domain.

In both January and October of 1523 disputations with papal representatives were held before large audiences in which Zwingli's knowledge of the Scriptures dominated and greatly impressed the local clergy and city officials, who came out in his support. In 1524, Zwingli sealed his break with Catholicism by marrying Anne Meyer Reinhard in the cathedral and reaching the conclusion that Holy Communion had purely symbolic meaning.[41] This also resulted in a complete break with Lutheranism, because Luther believed in the 'real presence'; although not in the full Catholic doctrine of transubstantiation. In 1525 the

Catholic Mass was suppressed in Zurich and paintings and images were removed from churches, which were whitewashed.[42]

Zwingli sincerely hoped for reconciliation with Luther and unity with Lutheranism. Philip of Hesse organised a Colloquy, which was held in the castle at Marburg in 1529. This major talk-fest lasted three days with Luther and Melanchthon representing one opinion and Zwingli and his friends, Bucher and Oecolampadius, the other. The parties agreed on fourteen out of the fifteen propositions that Luther had drawn up but they could not reach agreement on the nature of the Eucharist.[43] The only real outcome of this gathering was that Luther and Melanchthon went away and formalised their doctrinal position, publishing the famous creed of faith, the *Augsburg Confessions* of 1530, which, since then, has remained basic to Lutheranism.

As noted, the Anabaptist movement arose in the 16th century; a time of great religious turmoil. In 1525 the first known adult baptism of modern times was performed by Conrad Grebel near Zurich, virtually as a protest against his mentor,[44] Zwingli's, reluctance to institute reforms.[45] Zwingli had withdrawn his support for the Anabaptists and for rebaptism[46] and *"refused to accept their strict Biblicalism and doctrine of a free, confessional church."*[47] The Anabaptists disagreed with Zwingli's belief that baptism was similar to circumcision: membership of a religion. They interpreted baptism as a symbol of a person's regeneration, faith and future obedience to Jesus Christ.[48]

At first Zwingli saw no point in baptising infants who knew neither good nor evil, except if they were close to death.[49] He disputed with the Anabaptists and had greater difficulty with them than with the Papists because Anabaptists were radical and unshakable. Zwinglians turned against Anabaptists, persecuting the Swiss Brethren so that Zwingli did not object when the Council of Zurich beheaded one of them and drowned two others.[50]

From 1525, Balthasar Hübmaier was one of the leaders of the Swiss Brethren in Zurich who, even before he became an Anabaptist, had written, "*the burning of heretics is an invention of the devil*".[51] Hübmaier and Conrad Grebel were the first to determine the congregational form of government and, when Hübmaier resigned as priest of his congregation, they reelected him as their minister.[52] Hübmaier had been a friend and student of Zwingli, but the latter imprisoned him, forcing him to recant. Hübmaier fled to Moravia but was extradited to Austria and burnt to death in Vienna on March 10, 1529.[53]

Clearly, not all Protestants in Switzerland agreed with Zwinglianism and in October, 1531, five of the Swiss canons (called the Forest Canons) that dissented from his views mounted a sudden armed attack. Zwingli always carried a sword. Being the chaplain of his army, he also carried the banner, which made him a target. He died in battle on October 11, at the age of forty-seven.

Chapter 4

John Calvin (1509-1564)

When John Calvin (1509-1564), the son of Jeanne el Franc and Gérard Cauvin, a lawyer and/or the secretary to the Bishop of Noyon, was born in France his name was Jean Cauvin. His mother gave birth to at least seven children and died during Jean's childhood. Calvin was a deeply spiritual child whose father tried to steer him towards a career in the law but whose natural talent and inclinations prevailed. When he was twelve years old he became chaplain at the Cathedral of Noyon and was tonsured. In 1523 he attended the College de la Marche in the University of Paris where Erasmus had studied. There he learnt Latin before studying Law in Orléans, graduating in 1531. He went on to become a jurist.[54]

When Calvin heard a sermon preached by the rector of his Parisian church, Nicholás Cop, the young student was introduced to the ideas of Martin Luther. Calvin was totally converted but Cop had to leave Paris for Basel, in Switzerland.

John's studies led him to humanism and then he became a reformer, breaking with Rome in 1533 after receiving a vision which involved a call to reform the church.[55] He, too, fled from Paris to Angoulême in 1534 because of a crackdown on Protestants and the following year he, also, settled in Basel where he made contact with Cop and clarified his beliefs.

Plate 4.1. John Calvin 1550. Public domain.

Calvin visited Paris for the last time in 1536 and then went into exile in Geneva, Switzerland, where he completed his famous multi-volume *"Institutes of the Christian Religion"*. The first edition (in Latin) was completed in 1536 and he constantly refined it, editing it for the final time in 1559.[56]

In Geneva Calvin met the Protestant Guillaume Farel who persuaded him to stay and Calvin was elected to the office of preacher. He lived in Geneva for two years and many Roman Catholic clerics defected. Catholicism was banned and strict rules were beginning to be implement by the Council, but Calvin was opposed by a group that, strangely, was composed of Catholics and Libertines and he and Farel were banished in 1538. In Strasbourg Calvin married Idelette de Bure, in 1540, but their only child did not survive. Idelette died in 1549. In 1541 John Calvin was invited back to Geneva to help reform morals and behaviour with the full support of city officials.[57]

In Geneva, Calvin instituted the following reforms in churches: attendance was compulsory; there was a four-fold ministry (pastors, teachers, elders and deacons) and they policed the behaviour of the public.[58] There were no candles, altars, saints, organs nor singing.[59]

Calvin instituted numerous reforms in society: swearing, gambling, alcohol, dancing, immodest dress, adultery, fornication, singing, writing immoral books, promoting Catholicism and criticising Calvin and church officials were banned. People's homes could be entered to enforce the rules and punishments began with fines, then banishment and even death. From Calvin's return to his death (1541 to 1564) seventy-six people were banished and fifty-eight were put to death. Calvin believed that the state and the church were inseparable and that the state should implement church law.[60]

Calvin and Luther were not at all alike: Luther was *"large, loud and rude"* but Calvin was *"thin, quiet and scholarly"*.[61] Both preached justification by faith only (*sola fide*), in Christ alone (*solus Christus*), which took place in an instantaneous transaction with God.[62] Confession of this principle became basic to Protestantism. Calvin's theology and praxis were more radical than those of Luther and they paved the way for the restrictions of behaviour for which Puritanism is noted: for example dancing and games were forbidden in Geneva[63] so that it became a *"theocratic regime of enforced, austere morality"*.[64] Calvin is remembered for the doctrine of predestination: that the elect were chosen by God to be saved and could do nothing to change that; although all people should worship God.[65] The term 'Reformed' came to be attached to Calvinism only, and not Lutheranism.

Calvin's thorough education enabled him think through and analyse competing propositions and to explain Christianity clearly. Calvin's second period of political control in Geneva had begun in 1541 and the Scot, John Knox, arrived in the city in 1554. The following chapter will explain Calvin's working relationship with Knox.

In 1559 Calvin founded the Genevan Academy to train students for ministry in Reformed churches. It first rector was Theodore Beza who had previously been professor of Greek at Lausanne University and he became John Calvin's successor and biographer.[66] In 1558 Calvin he had contracted malaria but continued to wear himself out with frenetic preaching, debating and writing. At the end he was in considerable trouble with his liver and urinary tract and was fifty-four years old in 1564 when he 'went to God'.[67]

Calvin's great work was his *Institutes of the Christian Religion* which he kept on revising through many editions. It is still a classic. Calvinism is one of the primary and enduring stands of Protestant theology. It became strong in Switzerland and the Netherlands and was basic to the Scottish Presbyterians, the French Huguenots and the English Puritans.[68]

Chapter 5

John Knox (1513-1572)

5.1. John Knox in Scotland, Geneva and in Scotland again

John Knox (1513-1572) was born and died in Scotland but spent years in other countries. He was ordained in Scotland. He embraced the Reformation in about 1547, the year in which he was captured or sentenced to be a galley-slave for the French. In 1559, after he was released (or ransomed by the English) he remained in London. In 1531, being a priest he became a chaplain to the boy-king Edward VI and helped revise Cranmer's *Book of Common Prayer* but, when Mary Tudor became Queen of England in 1553, he fled to Frankfurt and then to Geneva.[69]

Plate 5.1. John Knox. Public domain.

5.2. John Calvin and John Knox in Geneva

When John Knox met John Calvin in Geneva in 1554 Knox became Calvin's disciple and a close friendship developed. With the consent of the town council in Geneva, Calvin invited Knox to help oversee public morality.

John Knox completed the transformation of Geneva into a hub of Protestantism and a refuge for European Protestant refugees, such as the hundreds who fled from the Roman Catholic Queen Mary Tudor of England. Geneva was not a paradise for all, however, as some critics of the harsh behavioural expectations and social control measures were tortured and executed there. [70]

Both John Calvin and Martin Luther, preached justification by faith only (*sola fide*), in Christ alone (*solus Christus*), which happened in an instantaneous transaction with God,[71] and which became the basis for the Protestant Reformation. Calvinism was, however, more radical than Lutheranism in doctrine and praxis, which paved the way for the strictures of Puritanism: for example games and dancing were forbidden in Geneva.[72] Under John Knox, Geneva became a "*theocratic regime of enforced, austere morality*"[73] which matched what Zwingli had done in Zurich.

5.3. Knox and Women in Authority

In 1557/58 Knox had written the pamphlet "*the first blast of the trumpet against the monstruous regiment of women*" which attacked women in authority, which, according to him, was against both the law of God and natural law.[74] Knox preached against two Queens, who were also arch-Catholics: Mary Tudor of England and the French aristocrat, Marie/Mary of Guise (1515-1569).

Plate 5.2. Mary of Guise. Public domain.

When Marie/Mary of Guise married King James V of Scotland she became Queen of Scotland and moved from France to Scotland. She was a member of the prominent and powerful French Guise family who were Catholics and staunch opponents of French Protestantism. James V, who was her second husband,[75] died after only four years of marriage so she became queen-regent for her infant daughter, Mary Queen of Scots. John Knox attacked Mary of Guise but many years later he also clashed with her daughter, Mary Queen of Scots. When Elizabeth I became queen in England, however, Knox tried to eat humble pie:[76] but Elizabeth refused to let him even enter her kingdom.[77]

When it was safer to do so, Knox returned to Scotland. As Mary Queen of Scots was more conciliatory than her mother, when Queen Marie/Mary (of Guise) had died, Knox and five others wrote the *Scottish Confession*, which the Scottish Parliament ratified in 1560. This ended papal control of Scotland but was itself replaced by the *Second Scottish Confession* or *Scottish Covenant*, in 1581, which was an even more anti-Catholic document. Calvinism was firmly established in Scotland by an act of parliament in 1592. When Mary married for the third time (to James Hepburn, Earl of Bothwell who had assassinated her second husband, Lord Darnley) the Protestant rite was used, which was denounced by the Pope.[78]

Plate 5.3. Mary Queen of Scots. Public domain.

John Knox was at the centre of political and religious turmoil in Scotland. George Wishart, a Scottish reformer who was his friend, was burned for heresy in 1546 by a Catholic Cardinal who was the Archbishop of St Andrews.[79] Another friend, James Stewart, Earl of Murray (or Moray) (who was interim regent of Scotland after the young Mary Queen of Scots was abducted to England) was murdered in 1570.[80] After his death Knox's political influence was reduced and Knox was never able to implement the puritanical reforms that Geneva adopted.[81]

Knox began his History of the Reformation in 1559 and completed it before he died, in 1572.[82] Knox had an able intellect and was an eloquent, logical preacher. He valued education, care of the poor and strict morality. He was considered outspoken, narrow-minded and bigoted but he valiantly stood up for his convictions.[83]

5.4. Conclusions

Along with Martin Luther, Ulricht Zwingli and John Calvin, John Knox was one of the leading lights of the Protestant Reformation, a period which has governed the direction and fate of the Church for five centuries.

The 16th century had been a time of political, social and religious chaos. Europe was wracked by wars in which politics and religion mingles and in which many thousands died. They became wars for power and influence and that power was demonstrated by the imposition of particular doctrines upon Christian people. Because of the Protestant Reformers, what had been the heavy fist of Roman Catholic domination of Europe began to lift in the 16th century because of a combination of some internal reform and greater external pressure. The Reformation prospered, as the politics of Scotland demonstrates.

Freedom of ideas also led to scepticism, individualism and anti-clericalism, which were in evidence in France during the French Revolution from 1789. This resulted in the semi-judicial killing of clergy, prelates, the aristocracy and the royal family and led to the secularisation of the country under Napoleon, although France has remained nominally Catholic. During the Middle Ages, secular trends had existed underground and emerged gradually, if and when the social climate thawed. The granting of choice in religion could, and often has, led to the complete rejection of religion, as has been obvious in Europe ever since.

Chapter 6

King Henry VIII (1491-1547)

6.1 Henry and the 'king's great matter'

Because King Henry VIII (1491-1547) had fallen in love with Ann Boleyn, who refused to be his mistress, Henry appealed to the Pope for an annulment of his marriage to his first wife, Catherine of Aragon, the mother of his daughter, Mary Tudor. Because the Papacy had originally granted Henry permission to marry Catherine (who was his teenage-brother's widow) it would have lost prestige by reversing that decision, so the Pope played for time. Henry and Catherine had been unable to produce a male heir, which the kingdom probably needed, and Henry claimed to believe that they were both under God's punishment for negotiating a forbidden marriage.

Henry's Vicar General, Thomas Cromwell, advised him to convene parliament and placed his predicament before it: advice which Henry followed in 1529. Parliament agreed to the separation of the Church in Henry's realm from Rome and to the establishment of King Henry as the head of the English church *"as far as the law of Christ allows"*.[84]

Henry VIII was an able and charming statesman who largely took the church, the parliament and the country along with him. The break with Rome was finalised by the passing of the following statutes:[85]

Submission of the Clergy (1532) - to Henry's will.

Restraint of Appeals (to Rome) (1533) - now forbidden.

Dispensations Act (1534) – No moneys to be sent to Rome.

Supremacy Act (1534) - Henry is supreme head of the Church of England.

Abolition of the Pope's Supremacy over clergy (1534).

6.2. Executions Under Henry VIII

In 1533 William Tyndale's friend, John Frith (1503-1533) was burned for denying transubstantiation and the doctrine of purgatory. In 1535 a number of Charterhouse monks and the scholarly Bishop John Fisher and Sir Thomas More were executed for denying the King's supremacy.[86] Henry dissolved 376 monasteries, ruining them and seizing their property.[87] In 1537, Henry permitted the English Bible (parts of which are attributed to Tyndale, Coverdale and others) to be sold to the public and (in 1538) to be available in every church, for parishioners to read.[88]

Henry was not a Protestant but he married Anne of Cleves to attract support from Protestant Europe. Despite the above Acts, Henry had no taste for radicalism and he went on to enact the *Six Articles* of 1539 which were popularly known as *"the bloody whip with six strings"*[89] largely to prove his orthodoxy. The *Six Articles* upheld the following Roman Catholic doctrines: communion with bread only, vows of chastity and widowhood, transubstantiation,[90] clerical celibacy,[91] private Masses and auricular confession (to a priest). Although Archbishop Cranmer had married Henry to Anne of Cleves he was prepared to divorce them because of his belief in the ultimate authority of the monarch. In 1540, Henry married Anne Boleyn's very young, poorly-educated cousin, Catharine Howard, who was not a Protestant (although his sixth wife, Katharine Parr, who outlived him, was).[92]

6.3. Outcomes

Although the Monarch of England would permanently replace the Pope, who excommunicated Henry VIII, Protestantism was not embraced until after his death but he laid the groundwork for it. He elevated Thomas Cromwell, Thomas Cranmer and many Protestant courtiers and, by encouraging the ordinary folk to read or hear the Bible in their own language, he changed the people's mindset so that they began to judge everything in the light of Scripture, as the reformers taught.

Chapter 7

King Edward VI (1537-1553) his regents

and his heir

After Queen Anne (Boleyn) was beheaded for adultery (which was considered treason) Henry VIII remarried and had a son, Edward, with Jane Seymour, his third wife who died almost immediately. Unlike his robust father, Edward was a frail boy but, at the age of nine, he became king as Edward VI (1537-1553). The Protestant Lords Protector (his maternal uncle, Edward Seymour, Duke of Somerset,[93] and John Dudley, the unscrupulous Warwick who became Duke of Northumberland) ruled in young Edward's name and set about introducing Protestant praxis and theology. They co-opted the Archbishop of Canterbury, Thomas Cromwell, who believed in the Divine Right of Kings, to implement the King's pleasure, introduced Thomas Cranmer's *Book of Common Prayer* in English (rather than the Latin Missal) and established the Church of England as the official church, but with Calvinist leanings. The work of Reformation in England could not be completed as Edward VI ruled for only six years.[94]

Plate 7.1. Prince Edward by William Scrots. Public domain.

John Dudley, Duke of Northumberland, had persuaded Edward VI to contravene Henry VIII's will and bequeath the throne to Edward's Protestant cousin, Lady Jane Grey, rather than to his Catholic half-sister, Mary, who (like the Lady Elizabeth) had been declared illegitimate by Parliament. Jane Grey had become a deeply convinced Protestant as, from the age of about fourteen, she had lived with Lady Elizabeth and Katharine Parr, Henry VIII's devout dowager queen, who married Thomas Seymour before she died in childbirth.[95]

Queen Jane Dudley (c.1536-1554)

When Edward VI was clearly dying the Duke of Northumberland (Dudley) wanted to marry his son, Guildford Dudley, to the Lady

Elizabeth but she wisely declined as she was beginning to sense danger in any marriage alliance. Jane Grey's parents, Henry Grey and Frances Brandon, the First Duke and Duchess of Suffolk, however, did consent to Guildford Dudley's proposal and bullied Jane, who disliked Guildford, into marrying him. Edward's half-sisters (Mary and Elizabeth Tudor) had both been declared illegitimate by Parliament but Jane, the oldest of the Grey's three daughters, was legitimate and was a granddaughter of Henry VIII's younger sister, Mary.

**Plate 7.2. Lady Jane Grey/Dudley.
Public domain.**

Northumberland persuaded King Edward, the Privy Council and the Archbishop of Canterbury, Thomas Cromwell,[96] to reject a Catholic queen (Mary Tudor) and to nominate Jane as Edward's heir by his valid will. In fact this by-passed not two but three other women who had a superior claim to the throne of England: Mary and Elizabeth Tudor (whom Parliament may reject an ineligible) and the arch-catholic, half-French, Mary Queen of Scots.[97]

When Edward died the matter was kept secret for two days, except from Jane who apparently said, "the crown is not my right and pleaseth me not. The Lady Mary is the rightful heir".[98] Jane, aged seventeen, was taken by barge, watched by a silent crowd, to the Tower of London where the crown jewels and royal apartments were made ready and her parents insisted that she obey them and comply.[99]

Jane was crowned in July, 1533, but never left left the Tower again. Nine days later the Privy Council had a change of heart and Queen Jane was ousted by spontaneous and popular opposition throughout the country. Jane (Grey) and her young husband, Guildford, had been pawns in a great anti-papist scheme. Mary Tudor, who ousted a crowned queen and assumed the throne in 1554,[100] delayed the execution of the newly-weds. In 1553, the Duke of Northumberland declared himself a Catholic and received the Catholic Eucharist, but Queen Mary still executed him. Some suggest that Dudley's motives when he presentation himself as a Protestant were either convenience, or greed for church lands.[101] His motive behind securing Queen Jane's coronation was his desire to become the real power behind the English throne.

Jane's father, the Duke of Suffolk, had been pardoned when he distanced himself from his daughter's cause and indeed he proclaimed Mary on Tower Hill[102] but when he became involved in Sir John Wyatt's Protestant rebellion against Mary, in 1544, his fate was sealed along with those of young Jane, and Guildford Dudley.[103]

Later, during Elizabeth I's reign, Jane Grey/Dudley was revered as a saint and martyr.[104] Jane was just one of many very worthy people whose lives were forfeited while the two opposite parties, Catholics and Protestants, were vying for control of the country.

Queen Mary Tudor (1516-1558)

Henry VIII's oldest child, Mary, had been raised as a devout Catholic by her Spanish mother, Catharine of Aragon. All of her youth she was her parents' only child and was loved by them. She was titled Princess of Wales by her father in 1525 and granted a court appropriate to her title. Her situation changed dramatically, however, when her mother was disgraced and replaced as queen by Anne Boleyn. Mary never saw her mother again, although they secretly corresponded. Mary suffered when, at about twenty years of age, she was forced to be lady-in-waiting to Anne Boleyn's child, her infant half-sister, the Lady Elizabeth. In 1536 Mary was forced to sign a document that acknowledged the illegitimacy of her mother's marriage and the supremacy of Henry VIII over the church and she was ordered to enter a convent, which she refused to do. Humiliatingly, she was known as the king's bastard and, for a time, she was excluded from the line of succession.[105]

Mary's relationship with Henry's third wife, Queen Jane Seymour, was an improvement as she was returned to court and was god-mother to her half-brother, Edward. King Henry's marriage to Jane Seymour was theologically uncomplicated (even for Catholics) because Anne Boleyn had been beheaded. Mary was also on affectionate terms with her father's sixth and final queen, Catharine Parr[106] who devoted herself to the education of the royal children and to nursing the king.

In 1552 there were sufficient Catholics among the population that Mary Tudor became queen (in place of Lady Jane Grey/Dudley) by popular acclaim. Mary's rule began by the repeal of Edward VI's anti-Catholic legislation. In 1554 Cardinal Reginald Pole arrived from the Pope to reconcile England with Rome, which was achieved in 1555.[107] Mary ruled with the help of her Catholic advisers, especially her Lord Chancellor, the Bishop of Winchester, Stephen Gardiner, until he died in 1555.

Plate 7.3. Mary Tudor. Public domain.

A year after becoming England's queen, Mary, whose mother had been Spanish, chose to marry the Catholic heir to the Spanish throne, Philip, although Parliament did not accept the marriage as it made England an adjunct to a foreign power and Spain, which was a great power, was viewed by the nobles with suspicion. This led to three simultaneous rebellions (in the Midlands, West and Kent) designed to replace Mary with Elizabeth and marry her to Edward Courtney. Only Sir Thomas Wyatt in Kent was able to raise an army (about 4,500 in total) but they could not take London, which was heavily defended at the gates and in the narrow streets. Some Thames River bridges were rendered useless and Courtney was arrested and interrogated. He confessed. So many were arrested that churches were used as jails and about 90 rebels were executed, including Wyatt and the Duke of Suffolk. Jane Grey and Guildford Dudley had nothing to do with the rebellion but they were also executed.[108] Mary won that round and married Philip.

Once Philip became the King of Spain, however, he returned home to Spain, although he came back to England in 1557 because he needed England's military help against France. Mary and Philip II successfully waged war together and were victorious at the Battle of St Quentin in 1557, but England lost Calais soon afterwards, which damaged Mary's popularity.[109] Their marriage, however, was neither successful nor fruitful, and Mary had a number of false pregnancies in her longing to have children.

In 1557, Cardinal Pole was ordained a priest and was immediately consecrated Archbishop of Canterbury in place of Thomas Cranmer, who had been excommunicated in November, 1555, and was burned at the stake in 1556.[110]

During Mary's five-year-long reign, and beginning with John Rogers, a canon (prebendary) of St Paul's Cathedral, three hundred Protestants would be burned as heretics. These included Bishops Nicholas Ridley and John Hooper, former bishop Hugh Latimer and Archbishop Cranmer, who are discussed below.[111] Many other Protestants died by hanging. The effect was *"an undying hatred of Roman Catholicism which became one of the most marked characteristics of the English for some 350 years"*.[112]

Mary Tudor's greatest desire was to see England returned to 'the True Faith'.[113] It has been suggested that she killed Protestants because she felt that *"she had not done enough to satisfy the judgement of God"*[114] but her motives may have been more complex. Certainly striking at leaders in order to cower their followers into submission was an old device. It was used, for example, by the persecuting Roman Emperors; so much so that, at times, being elected Bishop of Rome had been receiving a death warrant: although the courage of bishop-martyrs had the opposite effect during both eras.

The religious conflict in England reached its peak during Mary's reign especially as Edmund Bonner, Bishop of London was without pity.[115] Although a trained lawyer he, himself, beat stubborn witnesses with rods.[116] Many plots against Mary centred around Elizabeth, who had to be imprisoned in the Tower of London and would probably have been executed if Mary had produced an alternative heir. Mary's strict Catholic convictions, traumatic youth, unhappy marriage and childlessness combined to create five years of bloodshed in which hundreds of the most virtuous, pious and educated people and ordinary folk died violent deaths for their beliefs.

Chapter 8

John Hooper (c.1495-1555)

John Hooper, an only son, was born in Somerset, England and was sent to Merton College, Oxford University, from which he graduated with a B.A. in 1519. He became a friar: perhaps a Cistercian at Cleeve in Somerset.[117] As friars were not confined to the four walls of their monastery, Hooper worked in the service of Sir Thomas Arndell and was often at the royal court.[118]

After reading something of Zwingli, and his successor Heinrich Bullinger's commentary on St Paul's epistles, Hooper's conscience was pricked and in 1539 he departed for the Continent, having gathered what property he could (which was rather curious for a Cistercian as they embraced abject poverty). He married Anne of Tserclaes and then went to Zurich where he published numerous works and frequently met with Heinrich Bullinger, absorbing pure Puritanism.

Plate 8.1. Bishop John Hooper. [119]
Courtesy National Portrait Gallery.

After the death of Henry VIII John Hooper returned to England with many Swiss Protestant exiles, becoming their champion against Catholics and Lutherans alike. He became chaplain to the child-king's first Lord Protector, Edward Seymour, Duke of Somerset and so John Hooper found himself back at court and quite active in court politics. After Edward Seymour fell from grace Hooper became chaplain to John Dudley, Earl of Warwick (later Northumberland).

When Hooper had preached a series of Lenten sermons before Edward VI he was offered the See of Golucester but he refused to wear the prescribed vestments and to be consecrated according to the legally required rites. Archbishop Cranmer as well as Nicholas Ridley, Martin Bucer and others pleaded and cajoled. The King accepted his position but the Privy Council did not. He was called before them on May 15, 1550.[120] He was placed under house-arrest before he was incarcerated in the Fleet prison for weeks. A compromise was reached when, contrary to Cranmer's ordinances, vestments were to become *"things indifferent"* (*Res Indifferentes*) rather than articles of faith. Hooper was consecrated n March 8, 1551.[121] It is said that Hooper struggled with Archbishop Cranmer over the issue of clerical vestments until Ridley persuaded him to compromise[122] but it seems that both sides compromised.

Hooper was an active and energetic person and as the new bishop he visited his parishes, only to find an abysmal theological ignorance among the 311 clergy, some of whom could not say the Lord's prayer in English, much less the Ten Commandments. The *Articles of the Church of England* (numbers 9 and 10) stipulated that clergy *"were to teach the parishoners the Ten Commandments the Creed and the Lord's prayer as they were written"* and *"that every parson teach the Ten Commandments out of the tenth chapter of Exodus as they stand there and no (sic.) otherwise"*.[123]

Although Bishop Hooper attempted remediation, within a year Gloucester was downgraded to an archdeaconry and absorbed into the see of Worcester. Hooper became its bishop but with double the workload.[124]

Bishop Hooper was a genuine puritan: sincere, obstinate, bad mannered, devoted to small points and utterly confident in his conscience and his own judgement.[125] He had an unusual sensitivity for the needs of the poor and a concern for social justice.[126] His writings were widely disseminated after his death and were important in the spread of English Puritanism.[127]

Bishop Hooper disapproved of the plan to exclude Mary Tudor from the throne in favour of Jane Grey/Dudley but that did not save him. He was deprived of his See in March 1554 as a married man and was kept imprisoned in the Fleet "*on the doubtful charge of debt to the Queen although the real cause was his staunchness to a religion which was still by law established*".[128] As soon as the Heresy Acts could be passed, in December, 1554, he could be dealt with and, on January 29, 1555, with others, he was "*condemned by Gardiner and degraded by Bonner*".[129] He was sent to Gloucester where, on February 9, 1555, he was burned to death with great courage in front of his own cathedral, the first of the great martyred bishops of the English Reformation to die for their reformist beliefs.[130]

Chapter 9

Hugh Latimer (c.1485-1555)

The year of Hugh Latimer's birth in Leicestershire England is uncertain, but he was the son of a yeoman who rented his farm, ran 150 sheep and prospered sufficiently to give his son a good education from a young age. Hugh went up to Cambridge in c.1505, being elected a fellow of Clare College in 1509. He was awarded B.A. in 1510 and an M.A. in 1514 and then a B.D. He was *as obstinate a Papist as any in England* and had taken holy orders while at Cambridge. At his graduation in Divinity Latimer presented an oration against the Reformer, Philip Melanchthon, which had a curious result. His friend, Thomas Bilney, rushed to his study asking, *for God's sake hear my confession*, an incident which changed Latimer's life because Bilney's 'confession' was a testimony to his reformist beliefs.

Now Thomas Bilney was the leader of a group of Cambridge men who were influenced by Martin Luther and, through their friendship, Hugh Latimer was progressively influenced towards Protestantism. In 1527 Thomas Bilney incurred the displeasure of Cardinal Thomas Wolsey, *"and did humiliating penance for his offences"*.[131] In 1531, Thomas Bilney was burnt at the stake and Latimer penned, *"if such as he shall die evil, what shall become of me?"*[132]

Plate 9.1.

Hugh Latimer. Public domain.[133]

Although Latimer had become such a noted preacher that Cambridge University granted him a license to preach anywhere in England,[134] in 1525 he was forbidden to preach by the Bishop of Ely because he declined to preach a sermon against Martin Luther. With his quick wit and skilful argument, however, Latimer skilfully defended himself before Cardinal Wolsey, who restored his open license.

In 1530, Latimer preached before Henry VIII who approved and appointed him a vicar in West Kingston, Wiltshire, in 1531. He became a friend of Thomas Cromwell (later the king's chief minister) and Thomas Cranmer (later, from 1553, the Archbishop of Canterbury). These two tried to protect Latimer but in March, 1532, he was censured by a convocation of bishops for preaching heresy. He was excommunicated and imprisoned, before making a full submission.[135] The King intervened and he was released after conceding that he had erred.[136]

When Henry VIII broke with Rome, in 1534, Latimer became one of the Henry's chief advisors, along with Thomas Cromwell and Thomas Cranmer, advising him on the legislation needed to seal Henry's repudiation of the Pope, making it final and irrecovcable.

In 1535 Latimer became Bishop of Worcester. He preached at the burning of Friar John Forest, vainly trying to persuade him to submit to Henry's Act of Succession. He supported the king in the dissolution of the monasteries and the killing of the mother and family of Cardinal Reginald Pole (1500-1558) under Henry's Act of Attainder (a censure that Queen Mary Tudor removed).[137] From 1539 to 1540 Latimer's position deteriorated as he refused to agree to Henry's *Six Articles*, which, as noted above, upheld Roman Catholic doctrine on transubstantiation, vows of chastity and widowhood, communion with bread only, clerical celibacy, private Masses and auricular confession (to a priest). Latimer resigned his see in 1539 and, when Thomas Cromwell's head fell in July 1540,[138] he lost his main supporter, and spent time under house arrest and/or in the Tower of London; until Edward VI came to the throne.

Once Protestantism came out of the shadows, so did Latimer. No longer a bishop, by choice, but *"an orator in full vigour"*,[139] he continued to travel widely and preached powerfully in language that the crowds of ordinary folk enjoyed. Edward VI's six-year long reign were Latimer's years of fruit-bearing as his beliefs had matured and his cheerful, rough and playful oratory, with its touches of irony, was at its best. When King Edward died 'old Latimer'[140] could have fled but he did not try.

Queen Mary Tudor lost no time in summoning Latimer to Westminster and he cheerfully obeyed, aware that his end was near, knowing that "*Smithfield already groaned for him*".[141] He was tried for heresy at Oxford and burned to death with Bishop Nicholas Ridley on October 16, 1555. His final words to his friend Ridley have become immortal:

"*Be of good comfort, Master Ridley, and play the man; we shall this day, light such a candle by God's grace in England as (I trust) shall never be put out*".[142]

Chapter 10

Nicholas Ridley (c.1503-1555)

Nicholas Ridley, the second son of Christopher Ridley, was from a prominent family in Northumberland, England. He was educated at Royal Grammar School, Newcastle, and Pembroke College, Cambridge University. He graduated with a Master's degree in 1525. He was ordained a priest and then went to France to study at the Sorbonne in Paris and then Louvain. Upon his return c.1529 he gained a position at Cambridge, perhaps in the legal field, as, with his assistance, the university resolved on the matter of papal supremacy as follows:

> *"That the bishop of Rome had no more authority and jurisdiction derived to him from God, in this kingdom of England, than any other foreign bishop".*[143]

Nicholas Ridley then graduated with a Doctorate in Divinity (B.D.) in 1537 and became vicar of Herne, in Kent, but soon became a King's chaplain. He became a canon of St Paul's Cathedral in 1541 and of Westminster (in 1545). In 1540 he was elected Master of Pembroke Hall, Cambridge. Here he took a lead in *"transforming the university into a Reformist seminary that would soon contribute greatly to the intellectual life of English Protestantism".*[144]

Plate 10.1. Nicholas Ridley. Public domain.

After Ridley successfully fought off a charge of heresy he was appointed Bishop of Rochester in 1547. He began to radically change the interior of the churches in his see so that altars were replaced by tables: a very Protestant move.

In 1548 Ridley assisted Thomas Cranmer (later Archbishop of Canterbury) to complete the *Book of Common Prayer* to replace the Catholic Latin Missal. The following year Nicholas Ridley was one of the commissioners who investigated Bishop Stephen Gardiner of Winchester and Bishop Edmund Bonner of London before they were removed from office under Edward VI for refusal to accept 'royal supremacy' over the church. They were imprisoned and replaced by reforming bishops.[145] Bonner was replaced by Ridley, who made

London "*a showpiece of Reformed England*", whose introduction of plain tables caused an uproar.[146]

When Queen Mary Tudor ascended the throne Gardiner and Bonner were restored to their sees so Ridley had to be removed, and, as he had supported the claims of Jane Grey/Dudley, he was excommunicated. Once heresy was made a capital offence he was promptly arrested in July, 1553 and imprisoned. Nicholas Ridley, one of the finest academic minds of the Reformation, was taken to Oxford to be burnt at the stake with Hugh Latimer on 16th October, 1555.

Like Hooper and Latimer, Nicholas Ridley had a social conscience and he preached on social justice, even before Henry VIII, work which was connected with the founding of Christ's Hospital, St Thomas's Hospital and Bridewell.[147] Sympathy for the courageous deaths of the men of God, Latimer and Ridley, did much to stir the sentiments of English folk in the rural heartlands towards the Reformation.

1

Chapter 11

Thomas Cranmer (1489-1556)

Thomas Cranmer was the second son of a low-ranking squire in Aslockton, Nottinghamshire. He was educated at Jesus College, Cambridge, and he married Joan, an inn-keepers daughter, who died in childbirth within a year. While still a student, Cranmer was ordained to the priesthood and elected a Fellow of the College by 1523.[148]

Despite the dangers, William Tyndale, who had been in Cambridge from c.1515 to perhaps 1522 (before he went to Germany to meet Martin Luther in 1524) met with Thomas Cranmer and others to seriously consider the teachings of Luther and other Reformers so that they were known as 'Little Germany'.[149]

Cranmer, like many in that era, believed in the Divine Right of Kings: that the sovereign was given the throne by God. This and his great scholarship made him an idea servant to Henry VIII and Edward VI but it was a dangerous time as power was being contested by both the pro-Catholic and anti-Catholic factions, even during Henry VIII's reign; not to mention what happened after Henry's death.

Plate 11.1. Thomas Cranmer. Public domain.

When Henry VIII heard that Cranmer might support his desire to divorce his first queen, Catherine, he summoned Cranmer to court and *"ordered him to devote himself to writing up a Scripture-backed treatise in support of his right to a divorce"*.[150] As a consequence, when that queen's daughter came to the throne Canmer's fate was sealed. Mary Tudor had no intention of sparing the man who had declared her mother's marriage invalid. Cranmer had to die.[151]

In 1532, Cranmer had been sent by Henry VIII as an envoy to the Emperor Charles V and, while in Germany, he had secretly married a

German Protestant, Margaret Osiander, the niece of Lutheran Reformer, Andreas Osiander. All of the Reformers oppose compulsory celibacy but secrecy was essential, even in Henry's England.[152]

When the See of Canterbury became vacant King Henry appointed Thomas Cranmer to the position in March, 1533, which made the reluctant Cranmer the most powerful prelate in England. He obliged Henry by annulling his marriage to Catherine without recourse to the Pope and performed Henry's marriage to his latest love-interest, Anne Boleyn, who wanted to be his queen, not his mistress. Parliament, Thomas Cromwell (Henry's Vicar General), the Archbishop, and the King himself, all agreed that Henry's will should prevail in Henry's realm irrespective of the Pope's opinion. Between 1532 and 1534 legislation was passed to that effect, as noted in Chapter 6, above.

As Cranmer's personal views became more radically Protestant (perhaps under his wife's influence) internal conflict with his belief in royal absolutism increased as Henry's sentiments were still largely Catholic so that he only wanted to follow Protestantism far enough to achieve what he wanted: power and control, wealth from the monasteries he dissolved and the woman (or women) he wanted. Conveniently for Henry, Archbishop Cranmer pronounced annulments for Henry on his first two marriages to Catherine and Anne and his divorce from his fourth wife, Anne of Cleves, whom Henry married after his third wife, Jane Seymour, had died.

Protestants (and Cranmer) who had supported Henry were aggrieved when he enacted the *Six Articles* of 1539 (*"the bloody whip with six strings"*)[153] that upheld transubstantiation, vows of chastity and widowhood, communion with bread only, auricular confession, private Masses and especially clerical celibacy, as Cranmer was not the only cleric to have married. Indeed it was even rumoured that the Bishops of Winchester and York were married to women who were not free to marry.[154]

Two years after Cranmer had been tried for treason and heresy and had been excommunicated he signed a confession and a recognition of the Pope as vicar of Christ but he recanted and died bravely. Thrusting the hand that had signed the confession into the flames first he said, "*As for the pope, I refuse him as Christ's enemy and antichrist, with all his false doctrine*".[155]

Archbishop Cranmer is regarded as the Father of Anglicanism, having been the main author of the *Book of Common Prayer* and the compiler of the Thirty-Nine Articles (originally 42 articles) which governed how the church would function for the next five hundred years. His written work has been summarised as follows: he was responsible for the *Great Bible* (1538), the *Litany* of 1545 and two editions of the *Book of Common Prayer* (1549 and 1552), the *Reformation of Church Laws* (published posthumously in 1571), the *Articles of the Church of England*, the *Homilies* and the *Institution of a Christian man*.[156] Cranmer was a deeply thoughtful and deeply spiritual person, with a masterful command of the English language, but no other reformer had such struggles with their conscience trying to reconcile conflicting beliefs.

Chapter 12

Queen Elizabeth I (1533-1603)

Queen Elizabeth I (1533-1603)

In 1558, Elizabeth Tudor inherited from her Catholic half-sister Mary Tudor (1516-1558) a realm that had been torn apart by religious controversy and featured the deaths of many; luminaries and labourers alike.

Unlike both of her half-siblings Elizabeth I had a long life, from her birth in 1533 to 1603; and a reign of forty-four years. Having inherited a kingdom that was greatly divided along religious lines, after thirty years of turmoil, Elizabeth's long rule enabled her to calm the controversy; cement her position; successfully defy the Pope; break any connection with Spain left over from Mary's marriage to Philip II of Spain; defeat the Spanish naval armada (in 1588) and reconcile the populace to Anglicanism as 'the middle way'.

**Plate 12.1. Queen Elizabeth I: the Armada portrait.
Public domain.**

By 1559 Elizabeth I had implemented the *"Elizabethan Settlement"* which entailed the Act of Supremacy of 1534 (which re-established the status-quo which her father Henry VIII had devised) and the Act of Uniformity (of 1559) which, by a slim margin, passed though both Houses of Parliament.[157] Only one or two Catholic bishops agreed to take the Oath to Elizabeth so they were replace by those who would, which emptied the House of Lords of bishops who were hostile to her.[158] This made government much easier for Elizabeth, although many members in the House of Commons held Catholic sympathies. The removal of so many bishops raised the thorny question of whether the Apostolic Succession could be preserved in the ordination of new clergy and consecration of new bishops, such as for Canterbury, in 1559. Some who had been ordained bishop in the days of Henry VIII and Edward VI had survived Mary's reign and Anne Boleyn's chaplain, Matthew Parker (1504-1575) was consecrated for the See of Canterbury by John Scory, Miles Coverdale, William Barlow and John Hodgkin.[159]

By the "*Elizabethan Settlement*", weekly attendance at Church of England services was compulsory, as was use of the Church of England Prayer Book of 1552. Bible reading was promoted and Bibles were placed in churches. They were the Geneva Bible in English, translated by Protestants in Geneva, including Miles Coverdale (1488-1568) who had already completed an important translation of his own.[160] As noted, Bibles were readily available in the vernacular because of William Caxton's development of the printing press in 1477. When the Bible was read publicly each Sunday it helped ordinary folk to understand and absorb religious belief, not just rote learn it as they had previously and this facilitated the personalization of religious belief[161] so that parents could pray in the home in English and discuss theological issues with family and friends, referencing a Bible they could understand.

When Pope Pius V excommunicated Queen Elizabeth in 1570 she responded by suppressing the Catholic Mass and took stronger anti-catholic measures.[162] When a plot was discovered that involving her prisoner, her relative and heir, Mary Queen of Scots, Elizabeth reluctantly ordered that Mary be beheaded in the Tower of London on February 8, 1587. Mary Queen of Scots was the mother of the child James, who immediately became King James VI of Scotland and Elizabeth's heir. He later became the first king of the House of Stuart to sit on England's throne and he also retained the throne of Scotland. As James I he united the United Kingdom.

Elizabeth's policies utilised a mixture of both Henry's and Edward's innovations, which satisfied neither Catholics nor the extreme non-conformists who had come back from exile. All of Mary Tudor's pro-Catholic policies were reversed.[163]

With Elizabeth's accession the many Protestants who returned from exile in Europe were mostly Calvinists and/or strict Puritans. They gave Anglicanism a decidedly Calvinistic bent and constantly criticised Elizabeth's 'middle way' including anything of 'popery' such as clerical robes, making the sign of the cross and using written prayers.[164] Catholics and Dissenters (such as Puritans and Baptists) were suppressed, especially 'repeat offenders'.

The Church of England became the established religion and Dissenting Christians (Nonconformists) and Roman Catholics could be jailed under Elizabeth I's Act of Uniformity of 1559. Only members of the Church of England could vote, inherit property, own land, hold civil, parliamentary or military office or freely practise their religion.[165] Thus the Reformation did not solve every Protestant's problem as the Quakers, Puritans and Anabaptists would discover in the following century.

Conclusions

Elizabeth's refusal to marry, which earned her the popular title "the Virgin Queen" provided her with the ideology (which she capitalised on) that she was married to her people. She was clearly aware that staying popular was important, as was appealing to the largest cohort of people. Unlike her father, who fancied himself as a theologian, Elizabeth did not. She made measured religious decisions carefully, and cautiously avoiding extremes, aiming for the broad church that Anglicanism became. Acceptance of Elizabeth's 'Settlement' (by either the queen or the people) was based upon social and political considerations rather than any spiritual awakening or a quickening of religious convictions.[166]

Chapter 13

The Anabaptists and the Puritans

Modern day Baptists are loosely connected to the first Anabaptists. They arose in the 16th century as part of the great changes of the Protestant Reformation. Their martyrs were many. The origins of the movement are obscure because they were virtually an underground church that destroyed records to protect lives because so many thousands of their adherents faced danger and death. Their martyrs were the unknown shining lights of the era.

Because they were a congregational church Anabaptists avoided having a pope-like leader, such as Luther and Wesley virtually became to their own adherents. Every Anabaptist congregation had its own leader or pastor: local men who were not great bishops, university dons and scholars, but men who tried to keep a low profile to survive.

As noted in Chapter 3, above, the first adult baptism in the era took place in Zwingli's Switzerland in 1525 when Conrad Grebel baptised Georg Baurock in the home of Felix Manz, presumably by full immersion in a bathtub. Zwingli's own interpretation on baptism had changed in the course of his adulthood but he was not able to take all of Zurich with him, so that the Anabaptists, or Swiss Brethren, were Dissenters, even from dissent. Zwingli withdrew his support for rebaptism and came to believe that baptism, like circumcision, secured membership of a religion. The Anabaptists, however, interpreted baptism as a symbol of the candidate's faith, regeneration and obedience to Jesus Christ.[167] As a consequence of this fundamental difference Zwinglians turned against Anabaptists, persecuting the Swiss Brethren.

As noted above, in Zurich Balthasar Hübmaier led the Swiss Bretheren from 1525. He and Conrad Grebel were the first to determine the congregational form of government. When Hübmaier resigned as priest from his Catholic church, his congregation elected him as their minister.[168] He began as a friend and student of Zwingli but went beyond Zwingli in his reformist beliefs so that Zwingli imprisoned him and forced him to recant. Hübmaier then fled to Moravia but was extradited to Austria and burnt in Vienna on March 10, 1529.[169]

Anabaptist leaders were often martyred. Jacob Hutter was another. He led the Moravians, known as Hutterites, who held their property and children in common.[170] In Tyrol, Germany, Hutter had reported that 700 persons were executed, exiled or fled to Moravia, leaving their property and children behind, but they were expelled to Liechtenstein. Hutter, himself, was tortured and burned in 1536.[171] Another German, a former Lutheran preacher, Melchior Hoffmann (1500-1543) founded the Melchiorites or Hoffmannites in Germany and the Low Countries.[172] In 1533, he was sentenced to life imprisonment and died there, aged only forty-three.[173]

Michael Sattler, a Benedictine monk, became an Anabaptist after reading the New Testament. He preached in Strasbourg/Strassburg and Horb. *"Early Swiss and German churches owe their doctrinal and organizational stability to his work"*.[174] The King of Austria decreed a 'third baptism' for Anabaptists (i.e., drowning). In 1527, the charges against Sattler included that he had married. He defended himself by saying that marriage was ordained by God and that there was gross immorality among monks dend priests. His witness was steadfast and his death was noble, forgiving and pure. In 1528, Sattler was tortured and burned and his faithful wife was drowned.[175] Mass executions were common and, in Altzey, Anabaptists were hunted and executed on the spot; but they increased in number.[176]

Anabaptists did not have to adhere to defining beliefs and practices, but some ideas are common: the separation of church and state, adult baptism (or believers baptism) and a repudiation of infant baptism as erroneous and worthless, refusal to swear oaths or pay taxes,[177] a return to the New Testament church[178] in baptism and Holy Communion,[179] and withdrawal from the corrupt and evil society.[180] Holiness of life and love for the Word of God and were key characteristics.[181] All overt acts of sin were censured, including by shunning, but not by force.[182]

Anabaptists took the 'Great Commission' seriously. Of them, the Moravians/Hutterites developed the most extensive missionary work.[183] Many of them believed that the second coming would happen soon. Although some were pacifists, others, such as Hübmaier, believed in military service, if the government demanded it[184] and they fought valiantly against oppression.[185]

Puritanism, another aspect an individual's freedom to interpret the Bible, was closely associated with purity of life. In Geneva, John Calvin and John Knox controlled every aspect of life including dress, entertainment and family life. As noted in Chapter 4, above, gambling, alcohol, swearing, dancing, singing, immodest dress, fornication, adultery, writing immoral books, promoting Catholicism and criticising Calvin and church officials were all banned and punished with degrees of severity.

Naturally those English dissenting Christians who had fled to the Continent during the Tudor Period returned home influenced by some or other degree of Protestant conviction, so that the 17th century witnessed both trouble and even war with Puritanism, and the rise of Quakerism, which was a new, banned, variety of Christian belief.

Chapter 14

Conclusions

What a period of turmoil!

The Reformation was a seismic shift in the state of the Church, but only in the West; the Latin Church. The Eastern Church had had its own turmoil, but that's another story. The starting point for the Reformation was the Bible, which was forbidden to the laity but secretly translated, printed and distributed. Before the Reformation many monks, priests and academics had been permitted to access the Bible and, as the climate for reform improved, they interpreted and courageously preached what they read in the New Testament, often in the public streets. They became the Shining Lights of the Reformation; and often paid with their lives.

If the Reformation had not started in Germany with Luther it would have begun somewhere else in Europe because there were so many able, educated Christians seeking truth in the 16th century. Enquiring minds were being educated in Renaissance thought and scholars like Erasmus, the quintessential Renaissance scholar, were still alive to debate with Luther, engage with Zwingli and teach Tyndale in England. Once the printing press had been invented knowledge could no longer be confined to the monasteries and the universal language of the educated, Latin, enabled ideas to move freely across Europe.

The Roman Catholic Church needed the Reformation because it highlighted how far Catholicism had departed from the New Testament in doctrine and praxis as well as how morally corrupt it had become. One has only to compare Pope Francis XVI with the majority of Renaissance and Reformation Era popes,[186] and to consider what the Second Vatican Council (1962-1965) grappled with, to see the differences; although perfection has certainly not been achieved. If no Protestant Reformation had happened the Latin Church would have become more tyrannical and more corrupt: but it cost so many courageous and dedicated people, the cream of Europe, their earthly lives. Sometimes the achievements of the Reformation pale in the light of the heavy cost to its shining lights and their friends, families and followers.

BIBLIOGRAPHY
PRIMARY SOURCES
REFERENCE WORKS

Bettenson, Henry, *Documents of the Christian Church* 2nd ed. (London: Oxford University Press, 1968).

Cross, F. L. and E. A. Livingstone (eds), *The Oxford Dictionary of the Christian Church*
(Oxford University Press: London, 1958/1968/1972).
Luther, Martin, *95: The Ideas That Birthed the Reformation* (New Kensington, PA.: Whitaker House, 2017).

SECONDARY PRINT SCOUCES

Blech, Benjamin, *Eyewitness to Jewish History*
(Hoboken, N.J.: John Wiley and Sons, 2004).
Clarke, C. P. S., *Short History of the Christian Church*
(London: Longmans, 1961).
Demanus, Robert, *Hugh Latimer: a biography*
(London: The Religious Tract Society, 1869).
Dowley, Tim (ed.), *A Lion Handbook The History of Christianity*
(Lion, 1990).
Elton, G. R., *England Under the Tudors*
(London: Methuen, 1959).
Estep, William R., *The Anabaptist Story*
(Eerdmans, 1963/1975)
Fisher, H. A. L., *A History of Europe*, Vol. II
(London, Glasgow: Collins, 1964).
Foxe, John, *Foxe's Book of Martyrs*
(1563/2014),
Grimm, J., *The Reformation Era 1500-1650*
(N.Y.: Macmillan, 1954/1959).

Hammond, Peter, 'John Wycliffe - The Morning Star of the Reformation', reformationsa.org/index.php/reformation/130-john-wycliffe-the-morning-star-of-the-reformation

Hill, Jonathanl, *Lion Handbook of The History of Christianity* (Lion Hudson, 2007).

MacCulloch, Dairmaid, *The Reformation* (London: Viking, 2003)

McManners, John, *Oxford Illustrated History of Christianity* (Oxford and N.Y.: OUP, 1990).

Mursell, Gordon (ed), *The Story of Christian Spirituality* (Oxford: Lion, 2001).

Nevinson, Charles (ed.), *The Later Writings of Bishop Hooper* (London: The Parker Society, 1852).

Oyer, John S., *Lutheran Reformers Against Anabaptists* (The Hague: Martinus Nijhoff, 1964).

Prescott, H. F. M., *Mary Tudor: The Spanish Tudor* (Phoenix, 1940/2003).

Renwick, A. M., *The Story of the Church* (London. IVF, 1958/1962),

Rittner, Carol, Stephen D. Smith and Irena Steinfeldt (eds), *The Holocaust and the Christian World* (NewYork: Continuum, 2000).

Stayer, James B., *Anabaptists and the Sword* (Lawrence: Coronado Press, 1972).

Tomlin, Graham, *Luther and His World* (Oxford: Lion Publishing: 2012).

Walker, Williston, *A History of the Christian Church* (Rev.) (Edinburgh: T & T Clark, 1959).

ELECTRONIC SOURCES

Amber, Jasmine, 'The Queen's Mother: Marie de Guise',
https://venerablevixens.wordpress.com/2015/09/08/the-queens-mother-marie-de-guise

'Anabaptists' by the editors of *Encyclopaedia Britannica.*
https://www.britannica.com/topic/Anabaptists[1]

Cavendish, Richard, 'History Today, 'John Calvin Dies in Geneva',
https://www.historytoday.com/archives/john-calvin-dies-geneva

David Bahn –Reflections.
https://davidbahn-reflections.com/2017/10/31/martin-luther-here-I-stand-speech/

Encyclopedia of World Biography Ca-Ch 'John Calvin Biography',
https://notablebiographies.com/ca-ch/Calvin-John.htm/

Encyclopedia of World Biography, 'Martin Luther Bioography',
https://www.notablebiographies.com/Lo-Ma/Luther-Martin.html

Encyclopaedia Britannica, 'Philippe Melanchthon,'
https://www.britannica/biography/Philippe-Melanchthon

Fairchild, Mary, 'Biography of Thomas Cranmer, First Protestant Archbishop
of Canterbury. Life and Legacy of the Architect of Anglicanism'.
https://wwwlearnreligions.com/biography-of-thomas-cranmer-4780199

Fairchild, Mary, 'English Bible Translator and Christian Martyr',
https://www.learningreligions.com/william-tyndale-biography-700000

Hanson, Marilee, 'Lady Jane Grey- Facts, Biography, Information & Portraits.'
https://englishhistory.net/tudor/relative/lady-jane-grey[2] February 1, 2015

---

1.   https://www.britnnica.com/topic/Anabaptists

History-biography. 'John Calvin'.
https://history_biography.com/john-calvin/

'Hugh Latimer (c.1490-1555)', in *Encyclopedia Britannica*, 11th ed. vol. XVI, 1910.
www.luminarium.org/ren/it/latimerbio.htm[3]

McEwen, James Stevenson, 'John Knox: Scottish Religious Leader', https://www.britannic.com/biography/John-Knox

'Nicholas Ridley (martyr): biography. Early years and advancement (c.1500-50)',
https://fampeople.com/cat-nicholas-redley-martyr

Penn, William, 'The Life of Margaret Fell',
https://www.ushistory.org/penn/margaret_fell.htm

Pollard, A. F., 'John Hooper Bishop of Gloucester' in *Encyclopedia Britannica*,

11th ed,vol. XIII, 1911. *Tudor Place*, 'John Hooper', tudorplace.com.ar/Bois/JohnHooper.htm

Post-classical history 'the Revolution takes Form',
https://erenow.net/postclassical/the-reformation-a-histopry-of-european-civilization-from-wycliffe-to-calvin-1300-1564/90.pnp [4]

Scott, Elizabeth, '*Anabaptists: Separate by Choice. Marginal by Force.*' (1995).
www.bibleciews.com/Anabaptists.ByChoice.html[5]

The Attempted Coronation,
https://www.ladyjanegrey.org/queen/index.html

The Editors of *Encyclopaedia Britannica*, 'Edmund Bonner', https://www.britannica.com/biography/Edmund.Bonner[6]

---

2.   https://egluishhistory.net/tudor/relative/lady-jane-grey

3.   http://www.luminarium.org/ren/it/latimerbio.htm

4.   https://erenow.net/postclassical/tyhe-teformation-a-hisyopry-of-european-civilization-from-wycliffe-tp-calvin-1300=1564/90.pnp%5BAccessed

5.   http://www.bibleciews.com/Anabaptists.ByChoice.html

6.   https://www.britannica.com/biograsphy/Edmund.Bonner

The Editors of *Encyclopaedia Britannica*, 'Henry Grey, Duke of Suffolk',
   https://www.Britannica.com/biography/Hentry-Grey-Duke-of-Suffolk

The Editors of *Encyclopaedia Britannica*, 'Nicholas Ridley English Bishop',
   https://www.britannica.com/biography/Nicholas-Ridley

The Reformation-Facts & Summary – HISTORY.com
   http://www.history.com/topics/reformation
   Trueman, C. N., 'The Religious Settlement of 1559'.
   Historylearningsite.co.uk
   Trueman, C. N., 'The Wyatt Rebellion of 1554', The History Learning Site, 17/3/2015. https://www.historylearningsite.co.uk/the-wyatt-rebellion-of-1554/[7].

---

7.   https://www.historylearningsite.co.uk/the-wyatt-rebelklion-of-1554/

[1] Thesis No. 59 of Luther's 95. Martin Luther, *95: The Ideas That Birthed the Reformation* (New Kensington, PA.: Whitaker House, 2017), p. 122.

[2] Peter Hammond, 'John Wycliffe - The Morning Star of the Reformation', [Accessed 28/8/2020]. reformationsa.org/index.php/reformation/130-john-wycliffe-the-morning-star-of-the-reformation

[3] F. L. Cross and E. A. Livingstone (eds), *The Oxford Dictionary of the Christian Church* (hereafter *ODCC*) (Oxford University Press: London, 1958/1968/1972), *s.v.*, Tyndale, William [Accessed 26/9/2020].

[4] Mary Fairchild, 'English Bible Translator and Christian Martyr', https://www.learningreligions.com/william-tyndale-biography-700000

[5] *Ibid.*

[6] *Ibid* and Cross and Livingstone (eds), *ODCC, op.cit., s.v.*, Tyndale, William

[7] Fairchild, 'English Bible Translator and Christian Martyr', *op.cit.*, online.

[8] Henry Bettenson, *Documents of the Christian Church* 2nd ed. (hereafter *DCC*)(London: Oxford University Press, 1968), pp. 260-68. Also *The Reformation – Facts & Summary – History.com* http://www.history.com/topics/reformation [Accessed 15/6/2017] but doubted by others, Dairmaid MacCulloch, *The Reformation* (London: Viking, 2003), p. 119.

[9] *Encyclopedia of World Biography*, 'Martin Luther Bioography', https://www.notablebiographies.com/Lo-Ma/Luther-Martin.html [Accessed 19/8/2020].

[10] Williston Walker, *A History of the Christian Church*, Rev. (Edinburgh: T & T Clark, 1959), p. 304.

[11] For example, Henry of Lausanne, Tancred of Antwerp and Peter of Bruys. John McManners, *Oxford Illustrated History of Christianity* (hereafter *OIHC*) (Oxford and N.Y.: OUP, 1990), pp. 209-11.

[12] Walker, *op.cit.*, p. 306.

[13] Such a practice had long been forbidden, but he paid the Pope well.

[14] By which living people could purchase a reduction of time in Purgatory, for themselves, after death, or for their deceased relatives.

[15] Post-classical history 'the Revolution takes Form', https://erenow.net/postclassical/the-reformation-a-histopry-of-european-civilization-from-wycliffe-to-calvin-1300-1564/90.pnp [8][Accessed 1/1/2020].

[16] Jonathan Hill, *Lion Handbook of The History of Christianity* (Lion Hudson, 2007), pp. 250-251.

[17] Graham Tomlin, *Luther and His World* (Oxford: Lion Publishing: 2012), pp. 88-9, 92, 94.

[18] MacCulloch, *op.cit.*, pp. 120-121.

[19] Post-classical history 'the Revolution takes Form', *op.cit.*, online.

[20] *Ibid.*, p. 124.

[21] *Address to the Christian Nobility of the German Nation, The Babylonian Captivity of the Church* and *The Freedom of a Christian*, *ibid.*, pp. 124-27.

[22] David Bahn –Reflections. [Accessed 9/9/2020].
https://davidbahn-reflections.com/2017/10/31/martin-luther-here-I-stand-speech/

[23] Bettenson, *DCC*, *op.cit.*, pp. 279-283.

[24] Walker, *op.cit.*, p. 309.

[25] Cross and Livingstone (eds), *ODCC*, *op.cit.*, *s.v.* Luther, Martin (1483-1546).

[26] Walker, *op.cit.*, *p. 313*.

[27] Benjamin Blech, *Eyewitness to Jewish History* (Hoboken, N.J.: John Wiley and Sons, 2004), pp. 156-9, citing Jacob Marcus, *The Jew in the Medieval World, A Source Book, 315-1791* (N.Y., 2000).

[28] Doris L. Bergen, 'Collusion, Resistance, Silence: Protestants and the Holocaust', in Carol Rittner, Stephen D. Smith and Irena Steinfeldt (eds), *The Holocaust and the Christian World* (NewYork: Continuum, 2000), p. 49.

[29] Walker, *op.cit.*, p. 308.

[30] *Encyclopedia of World Biography*, 'Martin Luther Biography',
https://www.notablesbiographies.com/Lo-Ma/Luther-Martin.html [Accessed 19/9/2020].

[31] *Ibid.*, pp. 316-17.

[32] *Encyclopedia of World Biography*, 'Martin Luther Biography', *op.cit.*, online.

[33] The Turks remained a threat until 1545, the year before Luther died, when they signed a peace with the Emperor.

[34] Cross and Livingstone (eds), *ODCC*, *op.cit.*, *s.v.*, Luther, Martin

---

8.   https://erenow.net/postclassical/tyhe-teformation-a-hisyopry-of-european-civilization-from-wycliffe-tp-calvin-1300=1564/90.pnp%5BAccessed

[35] Cross and Livingstone (eds), *ODCC, op.cit., s.v.,* Melanchthon, Philipp.

[36] 'Philippe Melanchthon', *Encyclopaedia Britannica,*
https://www.britannic.com/biography/Philippe-Melanchthon [Accessed 19/6/2017].

[37] This moderate Lutheran statement of belief is the primary document for Lutheran Churches. Some Calvinist Churches in Germany accept a modified version. It was published in 1531.

[38] Walker, *op.cit.,* p. 312.

[39] *Ibid.,* p. 306.

[40] Cross and Livingstone (eds), *ODCC, op.cit., s.v.* Zwingli, Ulrich (or Huldrych).

[41] *Ibid.*

[42] *Ibid.*

[43] *Ibid., s.v.,* Marburg, Colloquy of.

[44] William R. Estep, *The Anabaptist Story* (Eerdmans, 1963/1975), pp, 25-26

[45] 'Anabaptists' by the editors of *Encyclopaedia Britannica.*
https://www.britannica.com/topic/Anabaptists[9] [Accessed 21/6/2017].
Conrad Grebel (d.1526) baptised Georg Blaurock (d.1529) in the house of Felix Manz (d.1527). Harald J. Grimm, *The Reformation Era 1500-1650* (N.Y.: Macmillan, 1954/1959), p. 266. Grebel died of the plague in 1526.

[46] John S. Oyer, *Lutheran Reformers Against Anabaptists* (The Hague: Martinus Nijhoff, 1964), pp. 203-4; Estep, *op.cit.,* p. 14.

[47] Grimm, *op.cit.,* p. 266.

[48] Elizabeth Scott, '*Anabaptists: Separate by Choice. Marginal by Force.*' (1995), p. 3.
www.bibleciews.com/Anabaptists.ByChoice.html[10] [Accessed 7/7/2017].

[49] *Ibid.*

[50] C. P. S. Clarke, *Short History of the Christian Church* (London: Longmans, 1961), p. 276.

[51] Estep, *op.cit.,* p. 197.

[52] *Ibid.,* p. 191.

[53] Cross and Livingstone (eds), *ODCC, op.cit., s.v.* Hübmaier, Balthasar.

---

9.   https://www.britnnica.com/topic/Anabaptists

10.   http://www.bibleciews.com/Anabaptists.ByChoice.html

[54] 'John Calvin Biography', *Encyclopedia of World Biography Ca-Ch*
https://notablebiographies.com/ca-ch/Calvin-John.htm/

[55] Cross and Livingstone (eds), *ODCC, op.cit., s.v.* Calvin, John.

[56] McManners, *OIHC, op.cit.*, p. 258.

[57] Richard Cavendish, 'History Today, 'John Calvin Dies in Geneva',
https://www.historytoday.com/archives/john-calvin-dies-geneva [Accessed 10/
10/2020].

[58] 'John Calvin Biography', *op.cit.,* online.

[59] History-biography. 'John Calvin'.
https://history_biography.com/john-calvin/. [Accessed 9/9/2020].

[60] *Ibid.*

[61] Hill, *op.cit.*, p. 264.

[62] McManners, *OIHC, op.cit.*, p. 259.

[63] Cross and Livingstone (eds), *ODCC, op.cit., s.v.* Calvin, John.

[64] The Reformation-Facts & Summary – HISTORY.com
http://www.history.com/topics/reformation [Accessed 1/1/2018].

[65] 'John Calvin Biography', *op.cit.*, online.

[66] Tim Dowley (ed.), *A Lion Handbook The History of Christianity* (Lion, 1990),
p. 382.

[67] Richard Cavendish, 'History Today, 'John Calvin Dies in Geneva', *op.cit.*,
online.

[68] History-biography, 'John Calvin', *op.cit.*, online.

[69] James Stevenson McEwen, 'John Knox: Scottish Religious Leader', p. 1.
https://www.britannic.com/biography/John-Knox [Accessed 19/6/2017].

[70] Cross and Livingstone (eds), *ODCC, op.cit., s.v.*, Calvin, John.

[71] MacManners, *OIHC, op.cit.*, p. 259.

[72] Cross and Livingstone (eds), *ODCC, op.cit., s.v.* John Calvin.

[73] The Reformation-Facts & Summary – HISTORY.com
http://www.history.com/topics/reformation [Accessed 1/1/2018].

[74] James Stevenson McEwen, 'John Knox: Scottish Religious Leader', pp. 2-4.
https://www.britannic.com/biography/John-Knox [Accessed 19/6/2017].

[75] Mary had married Francis, the son of the French King, in 1558. He died in
1560.

Jasmine Amber, 'The Queen's Mother: Marie de Guise', https://venerablevixens.wordpress.com/ 2015/09/08/the-queens-mother-marie-de-guise
[Accessed 1/12/2018].

[76] Knox dedicated a commentry to her.

[77] Cross and Livingstone (eds), *ODCC, op.cit., s.v.* Knox, John.

[78] *Ibid* and *s.v.* Scottish Covenant.

[79] McEwen, *op.cit.*, p. 4.

[80] *Ibid.*, p. 5.

[81] Cross and Livingstone (eds), *ODCC, op.cit., s.v.* Knox, John.

[82] Gordon Mursell (ed), *The Story of Christian Spirituality* (Oxford: Lion, 2001), pp. 178-79.

[83] Cross and Livingstone (eds), *ODCC, op.cit., s.v.* Knox, John.

[84] *The Act of Supremacy*, 1534, Bettenson, *DCC, op.cit.*, p. 318.

[85] Bettenson, *DCC, op.cit.*, pp. 305-321.

[86] Walker, *op.cit.*, pp. 359-61.

[87] *The Reformation – Facts & Summary – History.com, op.cit.,* online.

[88] Dates from Walker, *op.cit.*, p. 361. See also Cross and Livingstone (eds), *ODCC, op.cit., s.v.* English Bible, venacular.

[89] Bettenson, *DCC, op.cit.*, pp. 328-9.

[90] This doctrine holds that the elements (bread and wine) do become the body and blood of Christ.

[91] Even Archbishop Thomas Cranmer was forced, reluctantly, to 'put away' his wife in 1539 under Henry VIII's *Six Articles*. The Church of England abolished clerical celibacy in 1549 under Edward VI. Cranmer was martyred in 1556, under Mary Tudor (see Chapter 11).

[92] On 10/12/1541 Catherine Howard's early suitors, Dereham and Culpeper, were ececuted for high treason and, in 1542, Catherine Howard was executed without trial under a new law, retrospectively applied, that made it illegal for a queen to conceal her sexual history to the king.

[93] Somerset was executed in 1552 for mismanagement.

[94] Cross and Livingstone (eds), ODCC, op.cit., s.v., Cvranmer, Thomas [Accessed 10/10/2020].

[95] Marilee Hanson, 'Lady Jane Grey- Facts, Biography, Information & Portraits.' https://englishhistory.net/tudor/relative/lady-jane-grey[11] February 1, 2015 [Accessed 14/3/2019].

[96] So Cross and Livingstone (eds), *ODCC, op.cit., s.v.,* Cranmer, Thomas [Accessed 10/10/2020].

[97] Walker, *op.cit.,* 365.

[98] *The Attempted Coronation,* https://www.ladyjanegrey.org/queen/index.html [Accessed 6/6/2020].

[99] *Ibid.*

[100] Hanson, 'Lady Jane Grey- Facts, Biography, Information & Portraits,' *op.cit.,* online.

[101] G. R. Elton, *England Under the Tudors* (London: Methuen, 1959), p. 210.

[102] Elton, *op.cit.,* p. 213.

[103] The Editors of Encyclopaedia Britannica, 'Henry Grey, Duke of Suffolk', https://www.Britannica.com/biography/Hentuy-Grey-Duke-of-Suffolk[12] [Accessed 10/10/2020].

[104] Hanson, 'Lady Jane Grey- Facts, Biography, Information & Portraits,' *op.cit.,* online.

[105] Cross and Livingstone (eds), *ODCC, op.cit., s.v.,* Mary Tudor.

[106] *Ibid.*

[107] H. A. L. Fisher, *A History of Europe,* Vol. II (London, Glasgow: Collins, 1964), pp, 525-26.

[108] C.N. Trueman, 'The Wyatt Rebellion of 1554', historylearningsite.co.uk The History Learning Site, 17/3/'15. https://www.historylearningsite.co.uk/the-wyatt-rebellion-of-1554/[13] [Accessed 17/10/2020].

[109] Cross and Livingstone (eds), *ODCC, op.cit., s.v.,* Mary Tudor.

[110] Walker, *op.cit.,* p. 366.

[111] *Ibid.,* p. 365.

[112] Elton, *op.cit.,* p. 220.

[113] *Ibid.,* p. 215.

---

11.   https://egluishhistory.net/tudor/relative/lady-jane-grey

12.   https://www.nritannica.com/biography/Hentuy-Grey-Duke-of-Suffolk

13.   https://www.historylearningsite.co.uk/the-wyatt-rebelklion-of-1554/

[114] Walker, *op.cit.,* p. 366.

[115] Blaming Bishop Bonner shifted blame away from Queen Mary. At the time that Fox wrote this inditement Mary's half-sister, Elizabeth, was the queen.

[116] According to a contemporary source: John Foxe, *Foxe's Book of Martyrs* (1563/2014), pp. 248f of the 2014 edition. Foxe's opinion of Bonner is contested by The Editors of Encyclopaedia Britannica, 'Edmund Bonner', https://www.britannica.com/biography/Edmund.Bonner[14] [Accessed 17/10/2020].

[117] The Cistercians were founded in 1098 in France as an order of strict austerity and simplicity, but following St Benedict's rule. It was promoted by St Bernard (1090-1153) whose mystical contemplation of Christ impressed both Luther and Calvin, Walker, *op.cit.,* pp. 222-226.

[118] A. F. Pollard, 'John Hooper Bishop of Gloucester 'excerpted from *Encyclopedia Britannica,* 11th ed,vol. XIII, 1911. *Tudor Place,* 'John Hooper', tudorplace.com.ar/Bois/JohnHooper.htm [Accessed 10/10/ 2020].

[119] Courtesy National Portrait Gallery.

[120] 'Nicholas Ridley (martyr): biography. Early years and advancement (c.1500-50)',
   https://fampeople.com/cat-nicholas-redley-martyr [Accessed 17/10/2020].

[121] *Ibid.*

[122] Elton, *op.cit.,* p. 211.

[123] Charles Nevinson (ed.), *The Later Writings of Bishop Hooper* (London: The Parker Society, 1852), pp. 151 and 132-33.

[124] *Tudor Place, op.cit.,* online.

[125] Elton, *op.cit.,* p. 211.

[126] H. F. M. Prescott, *Mary Tudor: The Spanish Tudor* (Phoenix, 1940/2003)

[127] *Tudor Place, op.cit.,* online.

[128] *Ibid.*

[129] *Ibid.*

[130] *Ibid.*

[131] 'Hugh Latimer (c.1490-1555)', excerpted from *Encyclopedia Britannica,* 11th ed. vol. XVI, 1910.
   www.luminarium.org/ren/it/latimerbio.htm[15] [Accessed 19/9/2020].

---

14.   https://www.britannica.com/biograsphy/Edmund.Bonner

[132] *Ibid.*

[133] Robert Demanus, *Hugh Latimer: a biography*; (London: The Religious Tract Society, 1869).

[134] Cross and Livingstone (eds), *ODCC, op.cit., s.v.*, Latimer, Hugh.

[135] *Ibid.*

[136] 'Hugh Latimer (c.1490-1555)', ex. *Encyclopedia Britannica*, 11th ed. vol. XVI, *op.cit.*, online.

[137] Cross and Livingstone (eds), *ODCC, op.cit., s.v.*, Pole, Reginald.

[138] This was mainly because Cromwell had arranged for Henry to marry the Protestant German princess, Anne of Cleeves, with whom, when she arrived, Henry was disgusted.

[139] 'Hugh Latimer (c.1490-1555)', ex.*Encyclopedia Britannica*, 11th ed. vol. XVI, *op.cit.*, online.

[140] Latimer may have been born in 1470, in which case he was 90 years old, not 70. *Ibid.*

[141] *Ibid.*

[142] *Ibid.*

[143] Cited in 'Nicholas Ridley (martyr): biography. Early years etc., *op.cit.*, online.

[144] 'Nicholas Ridley English Bishop', The Editors of *Encyclopaedia Britannica*, https://www.britannica.com/biography/Nicholas-Ridley [Accessed 17/10/2020].

[145] Cross and Livingstone (eds), *ODCC, op.cit., s.v.*, Gardiner, Stephen 1490-1555.

[146] 'Nicholas Ridley English Bishop', *op.cit.*, online.

[147] Cross and Livingstone (eds), *ODCC, op.cit., s.v.*, Ridley, Nicholas.

[148] Mary Fairchild, 'Biography of Thomas Cranmer, First Protestant Archbishop of Canterbury. Life and Legacy of the Architect of Anglicanism'. [Accessed 10/10/2020].
https://wwwlearnreligions.com/biography-of-thomas-cranmer-4780199

[149] *Ibid.*

[150] *Ibid.*

[151] Walker, *op.cit.*, p. 366.

[152] Cross and Livingstone (eds), *ODCC, op.cit., s.v.*, Cranmer, Thomas.

---

[153] Bettenson, *DCC*, *op.cit.*, pp. 328-9.

[154] Elton, *op.cit.*, p. 211.

[155] Fairchild, 'Biography of Thomas Cranmer,' *op.cit.*, online.

[156] James Atkinson, 'Thomas Crannmer', in Dowley (ed.), *op.cit.*, p. 391.

[157] Elizabeth became 'Supreme Governor' of the Church, not 'Head'.

[158] C. N. Trueman, 'The Religious Settlement of 1559'. (hereafter 'Religious Settlement') Historylearningsite.co.uk [Accessed 6/8/2017].

[159] Walker, *op.cit.*, p. 167.

[160] A. M. Renwick, *The Story of the Church* (London. IVF, 1958/1962), pp. 130-132,

[161] Carke, *Short History*, *op.cit.*, pp. 321-325.

[162] Cross and Livingstone (eds), *ODCC*, *op.cit.*, *s.v.* Elizabeth I.

[163] *Ibid.*

[164] Trueman, 'Religious Settlement', *op.cit.*, online.

[165] William Penn, 'The Life of Margaret Fell', https://www.ushistory.org/penn/margaret_fell.htm
[Accessed 18/7/2017].

[166] Walker, *op.cit.*, p. 368.

[167] Elizabeth Scott, '*Anabaptists: Separate by Choice. Marginal by Force.*' (1995), p. 3.
www.bibleciews.com/Anabaptists.ByChoice.html[16] [Accessed 7/7/2017].

[168] *Ibid.*, p. 191.

[169] Cross and Livingstone (eds), *ODCC*, *op.cit.*, *s.v.* Hübmaier, Balthasar.

[170] Elizabeth Scott., *op.cit.*, p. 8, citing Claus-Peter Clasen, *Anabaptism: A Social History* (Ithca: Cornell University Press, 1972), p. 295.

[171] Estep, *op.cit.*, pp. 92-95.

[172] They are: the Netherlands, the Spanish Netherlands (Belgium) and Luxenburg.

[173] Cross and Livingstone (eds), *ODCC*, *op.cit.*, *s.v.* Hoffmann, Melochoir.

[174] Estep, *op.cit.*, p. 41

[175] *Ibid.*, pp. 46-47

---

16.   http://www.bibleciews.com/Anabaptists.ByChoice.html

[176] *Ibid.*, p. 49.

[177] *Ibid.*, p. 8.

[178] *Ibid.*, pp.1 and 6.

[179] *Ibid.*, p. 4.

[180] *Ibid.*, p. 5.

[181] Elizabeth Scott, *op.cit.*, p. 6.

[182] Estep *op.cit.*, p.187.

[183] *Ibid.*, p. 193.

[184] *Ibid.*, p. 192.

[185] James B. Stayer, *Anabaptists and the Sword* (Lawrence: Coronado Press, 1972), p. 28.

[186] Leo X was an exception, according to Luther's brochure *Resolutiones* (April, 1518). See Post-classical history 'the Revolution takes Form', *op.cit.*, online.

Also by Deslee Campbell

Memorable Christians

Phoebe's Sister's: Women Leaders in Early Christianity
Phoebe's Sisters : Women Leaders in Early Christianity
Bright Shining Lights of an Earlier Era
Shining Lights of the Reformation
Modern Christian Martyrs
Great Christian Men We Have Forgotten
Great Christian Men We Have Forgotten

Standalone

The Topkapi Beggar
Voices From The Silence
Why a Roman Emperor Rebuilt Jerusalem and Jerash
Stones, Walls and Watchmen
Mothers in Israel
Ecclesia a Long Journey to Tomorrow

Watch for more at www.synagogueandchurch.com.

About the Author

About the Author

Dr Deslee Campbell, a retired educational psychologist and teacher, is a prolific writer of both fiction and works concerned with history, religion and archaeology. She is particularly interested in art, artefacts and architecture as pathways towards understanding the past. Her doctoral thesis from the University of Sydney is entitled "The Iconography of Women: A Study of Byzantium and the Byzantine-influenced Mediterranean, A.D. 395-1204."

Read more at https://www.youtube.com/@synagogueandchurch911.